The Art of Fundraising , The Money Map: How to Attract Capital and Grow Your Business.

Frederic BEHE

Part 1: Introduction to Funding

In this section, we'll explore the critical role that funding plays in the success of any business, and introduce the different types of funding available to entrepreneurs and business owners.

Whether you're just starting out or looking to scale your existing business, securing the right type and amount of funding is essential for achieving your goals. Funding can provide the resources necessary to invest in marketing, research and development, hiring, and other key areas that drive growth and profitability.

But with so many different types of funding available, it can be challenging to determine which one is right for your business. In this section, we'll break down the pros and cons of each type of funding, including bootstrapping, traditional funding sources like bank loans and venture capitalists, and alternative funding sources like crowdfunding and government grants.

We'll also provide guidance on how to determine which type of funding might be best suited for your business needs based on factors like the stage of your business, the amount of funding you need, and the level of risk you're willing to take on. By the end of this section, you'll have a solid understanding of the different types of funding available and how to choose the right one for your business.

1.1 Why funding is crucial for business success

Funding is one of the most critical components of any successful business. It provides entrepreneurs and business owners with the necessary resources to grow and scale their operations, invest in research and development, and attract top talent to their team. Without adequate funding, businesses may struggle to achieve their goals and stay competitive in their industry.

There are several reasons why funding is so important for business success:

Funding enables businesses to invest in growth:

With access to funding, businesses can invest in marketing and advertising, product development, and other key areas that drive growth and profitability. This can help businesses stay ahead of their competition, reach new customers, and expand their operations.

Funding provides a safety net during difficult times:

In an ever-changing market, businesses may face unexpected challenges and downturns that can threaten their survival. With adequate funding, businesses can weather these challenges and continue to operate, ensuring their long-term success.

Funding allows businesses to take risks:

In order to differentiate themselves from competitors and establish a foothold in their market, businesses may need to take calculated risks. With access to funding, businesses can take these risks without fear of running out of resources, allowing them to pursue new opportunities and achieve greater success.

Funding can provide access to valuable resources:

In addition to financial resources, funding can also provide businesses with access to industry expertise, mentorship, and other valuable resources. This can help businesses make better decisions, avoid costly mistakes, and stay competitive in their market.

Overall, funding is essential for any business looking to achieve long-term success. By securing the right type and amount of funding, businesses can invest in growth, weather unexpected challenges, take risks, and access valuable resources. In the following sections of this book, we'll explore the different types of funding available and provide guidance on how to choose the right funding option for your business.

1.2 Different types of funding available

When it comes to funding a business, there are many options available. Each option has its own advantages and disadvantages, and the right choice will depend on the needs and goals of the business. Here are some of the most common types of funding available:

Personal savings:

Many entrepreneurs and small business owners choose to fund their ventures with personal savings. This can be a good option for businesses that don't require a large amount of capital upfront, and for individuals who are willing to take on personal risk.

Friends and family:

Another common way to fund a business is through loans or investments from friends and family members. This can be a good option for businesses that are just starting out, as it can be easier to secure funding from people who already know and trust the entrepreneur.

Crowdfunding:

Crowdfunding has become increasingly popular in recent years, with platforms like Kickstarter and Indiegogo allowing entrepreneurs to raise funds from a large number of individuals. Crowdfunding can be a good option for businesses that have a unique or innovative product or service that is likely to generate interest from a wide audience.

Angel investors:

Angel investors are typically wealthy individuals who provide funding to startups and early-stage businesses in exchange for equity in the company. Angel investors can provide not only funding, but also valuable industry expertise and connections.

Venture capital:

Venture capital is a type of funding provided by institutional investors, such as investment banks and private equity firms, to startups and early-stage businesses that have high growth potential. Venture capitalists typically provide funding in exchange for equity in the company, and may also provide mentorship and other resources.

Bank loans:

Traditional bank loans are another option for businesses that need to borrow money. Bank loans can be a good option for established businesses with a strong credit history, as they typically offer lower interest rates and longer repayment terms than other types of loans.

Grants:

Finally, businesses may be able to secure funding through grants from government agencies or non-profit organizations. Grants can be a good option for businesses that are working on projects with a social or environmental impact, and may not have the same profitability goals as traditional businesses.

There are many different types of funding available for businesses, each with its own benefits and drawbacks. By understanding the different options available, entrepreneurs can choose the funding source that best meets their needs and goals. In the following sections of this book, we'll explore each type of funding in more detail, providing guidance on how to secure funding and maximize its benefits for your business.

1.3 Pros and cons of each type of funding

As we discussed in the previous section, there are many different types of funding available for businesses. Each option has its own advantages and disadvantages, and the right choice will depend on the needs and goals of the business. Let's take a closer look at the pros and cons of each type of funding:

1. Personal savings

Pros:
- No need to pay interest or give up equity in the company
- Complete control over the business and its finances
- Demonstrates commitment and confidence in the business to potential investors

Cons:
- Limited funding available
- Personal financial risk if the business fails
- May not be enough to cover all startup costs

2. Friends and family

Pros:
- Easier to secure funding from people who already know and trust the entrepreneur
- Flexible repayment terms and lower interest rates than traditional loans
- Can be a good way to start building a network of supporters and investors

Cons:
- Personal relationships can be strained if the business fails
- Limited funding available
- Potential for misunderstandings or disagreements about the terms of the loan or investment

3. Crowdfunding

Pros:
- Access to a large pool of potential investors
- Can generate buzz and publicity for the business

- Minimal financial risk for the entrepreneur

Cons:
- Time-consuming and requires a significant amount of effort to create a successful campaign
- May not be an effective option for businesses that are not unique or innovative
- Fees and commissions charged by crowdfunding platforms can be high

---

4. Angel investors

Pros:
- Access to funding and industry expertise
- Can provide mentorship and connections to other investors
- Often more flexible than traditional lenders

Cons:
- May require the entrepreneur to give up a significant amount of equity in the company
- May require a lot of time and effort to find the right investor and negotiate a deal
- Can be difficult to find the right investor who is aligned with the business's goals and values

---

5. Venture capital

Pros:
- Access to significant amounts of funding
- Often comes with mentorship, connections, and expertise from experienced investors
- Can be a good way to rapidly scale the business

Cons:
- Often requires a significant amount of equity in the company

- Can be time-consuming and competitive to secure funding
- May require the business to meet strict growth targets and milestones

6. Bank loans

Pros:
- Lower interest rates and longer repayment terms than other types of loans
- Established banks can offer credibility and stability to the business
- Can be a good way to build a credit history for the business

Cons:
- Can be difficult to secure for startups or businesses without an established credit history
- May require collateral or a personal guarantee from the entrepreneur
- Repayment terms can be inflexible and may require a steady cash flow to meet payments

7. Grants

Pros:
- Free money that does not need to be repaid
- Can be a good way to fund socially or environmentally impactful projects
- Can add credibility to the business and demonstrate commitment to a cause

Cons:
- Can be difficult to secure due to high competition and strict eligibility requirements
- Limited funding available
- May require the business to meet specific reporting requirements or restrictions on how the funds can be used

There is no one-size-fits-all solution when it comes to funding a business. Each option has its own benefits and drawbacks, and the right choice will depend on the needs and goals of the business. By carefully weighing the pros and cons of each option and seeking expert advice, entrepreneurs can make an informed decision about which funding source is best for their business.

Part 2: Preparing for Funding

Before seeking funding for a business, it is important for entrepreneurs to take the time to prepare themselves and their business. This includes researching potential funding sources, understanding the requirements and expectations of investors or lenders, and developing a solid business plan. In this section, we will explore the key steps that entrepreneurs should take to prepare for funding, including conducting market research, analyzing financials, and creating a pitch deck. By taking these steps, entrepreneurs can increase their chances of securing the funding they need to turn their business ideas into reality.

2.1 Conducting market research

One of the key steps in preparing for funding is conducting thorough market research. This involves gathering and analyzing information about the target market, industry trends, and potential competitors. By conducting market research, entrepreneurs can identify gaps in the market, understand customer needs and preferences, and determine how their business can stand out from the competition.

There are several methods that entrepreneurs can use to conduct market research, including:

Surveys:

Surveys are a common method of gathering information from potential customers. Surveys can be conducted online, by phone, or in person, and can be used to gather information about customer demographics, preferences, and purchasing habits.

Focus Groups:

Focus groups involve bringing together a small group of potential customers to discuss a product or service. The goal of a focus group is to gather qualitative feedback about the product or service and to identify areas for improvement.

Secondary Research:

Secondary research involves gathering information from existing sources, such as industry reports, government publications, and competitor websites. This information can provide valuable insights into industry trends, customer preferences, and potential market size.

Once market research has been conducted, entrepreneurs should analyze the data and use it to inform their business plan and funding strategy. For example, if market research indicates that there is high demand for a particular type of product or service, entrepreneurs may choose to focus their funding efforts on developing and marketing that product or service. By conducting thorough market research and using the insights gained to inform their funding strategy, entrepreneurs can increase their chances of securing funding and achieving business success.

2.2 Developing a solid business plan

Developing a solid business plan is a critical step in preparing for funding. A business plan is a document that outlines the vision and strategy for the business, and includes details about the products or services offered, target market, marketing strategy, financial projections, and more. A well-developed business plan not only helps entrepreneurs to clarify their goals and strategy, but also serves as a roadmap for the business and a key tool for attracting funding.

To develop a solid business plan, entrepreneurs should consider the following key elements:

Executive Summary:

This is a brief overview of the business, including its goals, target market, and unique selling proposition. The executive summary should be clear and concise, and provide a compelling case for why the business is a good investment opportunity.

Market Analysis:

This section should provide an in-depth analysis of the target market, including demographic information, market size and trends, and competitor analysis. Entrepreneurs should use market research data to inform their analysis and identify opportunities and challenges in the market.

Products or Services:

This section should provide detailed information about the products or services offered by the business, including features, benefits, and pricing. Entrepreneurs should highlight the unique aspects of their offerings and explain how they meet the needs of the target market.

Marketing and Sales Strategy:

This section should outline the marketing and sales tactics that will be used to reach the target market and promote the products or services. Entrepreneurs should explain their marketing channels, customer acquisition strategy, and pricing strategy.

Financial Projections:

This section should include financial projections for the business, including revenue, expenses, and profit margins. Entrepreneurs should use historical financial data, market research, and industry benchmarks to inform their projections.

Management Team:

This section should provide information about the management team, including their experience and qualifications. Entrepreneurs should highlight the strengths of the team and explain how they are uniquely qualified to lead the business.

By developing a solid business plan, entrepreneurs can demonstrate their understanding of the market, their strategy for success, and their ability to manage finances and operations effectively. This can help to build investor confidence and increase the likelihood of securing funding.

2.3 Building a team with relevant experience

Building a team with relevant experience is a critical step in preparing for funding. Investors are typically looking for a team that has the knowledge, skills, and experience necessary to successfully execute the business plan and deliver on the promised results. As such, entrepreneurs should focus on assembling a team with the relevant experience and expertise needed to achieve their goals.

To build a team with relevant experience, entrepreneurs should consider the following key elements:

Define the Roles and Responsibilities:

Before hiring team members, entrepreneurs should clearly define the roles and responsibilities that are needed to achieve the business goals. This includes identifying the skills and experience needed for each role and setting expectations for performance.

Create a Job Description:

Once the roles and responsibilities have been defined, entrepreneurs should create a job description that outlines the qualifications, experience, and skills required for each position. The job description should be clear and concise, and include the key responsibilities and deliverables expected of the role.

Use Networking and Referrals:

One effective way to find team members with relevant experience is to use networking and referrals. Entrepreneurs can tap into their personal and professional networks to identify potential candidates, or ask for referrals from colleagues, industry contacts, or investors.

Screen Candidates Carefully:

When evaluating potential candidates, entrepreneurs should screen them carefully to ensure they have the required experience and qualifications. This may include reviewing resumes, conducting phone or video interviews, and conducting background checks or reference checks.

Hire for Cultural Fit:

In addition to evaluating candidates for their skills and experience, entrepreneurs should also consider their fit with the company culture. This includes assessing their values, work style, and personality to ensure they align with the company's mission and values.

Provide Ongoing Training and Development:

Once team members have been hired, entrepreneurs should provide ongoing training and development to ensure they have the skills and knowledge needed to succeed. This may include providing access to industry training or certifications, mentoring and coaching, or on-the-job training.

By building a team with relevant experience, entrepreneurs can demonstrate to investors that they have the talent and expertise needed to execute their business plan and deliver results. This can help to build investor confidence and increase the likelihood of securing funding.

2.4 Assessing the financial needs of the business

Assessing the financial needs of the business is a critical step in preparing for funding. Entrepreneurs must have a clear understanding of the capital required to launch and scale the business, as well as a detailed financial plan outlining how the funds will be utilized. This includes determining the funding required for working capital, equipment, facilities, inventory, marketing, and other operating expenses.

To assess the financial needs of the business, entrepreneurs should consider the following key elements:

Conduct a Comprehensive Financial Analysis:

Entrepreneurs should conduct a comprehensive financial analysis to determine the capital required to launch and scale the business. This includes estimating the initial capital required to start the business, as well as the ongoing capital required to support day-to-day operations and growth.

Develop a Detailed Financial Plan:

Once the financial needs of the business have been assessed, entrepreneurs should develop a detailed financial plan that outlines how the funds will be utilized. This includes creating financial projections for revenue, expenses, and cash flow, and identifying key milestones and metrics that will be used to measure the success of the business.

Identify Funding Sources:

After assessing the financial needs of the business and creating a detailed financial plan, entrepreneurs should identify potential funding sources. This may include angel investors, venture capitalists, banks, or other sources of capital. Each funding source has its own requirements and criteria for funding, so entrepreneurs should carefully evaluate each option to determine which is the best fit for their business.

Determine the Funding Structure:

Once potential funding sources have been identified, entrepreneurs must determine the funding structure that best suits their business. This includes evaluating the pros and cons of each funding option, negotiating the terms of the funding agreement, and determining the ownership and control structure of the business.

Prepare a Funding Proposal:

Once the funding structure has been determined, entrepreneurs should prepare a funding proposal that outlines the business plan, financial projections, and funding requirements. This proposal should be professional and well-researched, and should demonstrate a clear understanding of the business and its potential for growth.

By assessing the financial needs of the business and developing a detailed financial plan, entrepreneurs can demonstrate to investors that they have a clear understanding of the capital required to launch and scale the business. This can help to build investor confidence and increase the likelihood of securing funding.

Part 3: Bootstrapping and Self-Funding

Bootstrapping and self-funding are methods of financing a business that rely on the entrepreneur's own resources, rather than external sources of capital. These methods can be ideal for entrepreneurs who want to maintain control of their business or who may not have access to traditional funding sources. While bootstrapping and self-funding can be challenging, they can also be a great way to launch and grow a business without taking on significant debt or giving up equity to outside investors.

Part 3 of this book will explore the strategies and best practices for bootstrapping and self-funding a business. We will examine the benefits and drawbacks of these approaches, as well as the various methods that entrepreneurs can use to fund their business using their own resources. By the end of this section, you will have a solid understanding of how to bootstrap and self-fund your business and how to make the most of these strategies to achieve your goals.

3.1 Advantages of bootstrapping and self-funding

Retain control of your business:

Retaining control of your business is one of the key advantages of bootstrapping and self-funding. When you fund your business with your own resources, you have complete autonomy to make decisions and run your business as you see fit. This means you don't have to consult with external investors or answer to a board of directors, and you can make changes quickly and easily without seeking approval from others.
For some entrepreneurs, maintaining control is a top priority. They may have a strong vision for their business and want to ensure that it stays true to their original goals and values. They may also want to avoid

potential conflicts with outside investors who may have different ideas about how the business should be run or what its priorities should be.

In addition to providing more control, self-funding can also give you the freedom to pursue unconventional strategies or take risks that you may not be able to pursue if you were relying on external funding sources. This can be especially valuable if you're pursuing a new or untested business idea, or if you're operating in a highly competitive market where innovation is key.

It's important to note that retaining control does come with certain risks. When you're the sole decision-maker, you also bear all the responsibility for the success or failure of your business. If you make poor decisions, you may not have anyone else to turn to for help.

As your business grows, you may find that you need to bring on outside investors or partners in order to achieve your long-term goals. In these cases, you'll need to be prepared to give up some control in exchange for the resources you need to grow and succeed.

No debt:

Another advantage of bootstrapping and self-funding is that you can avoid taking on debt to finance your business. When you rely on external funding sources, you typically have to borrow money from lenders or investors, which means you'll need to pay interest or give up equity in your business in exchange for the funding you receive.
By contrast, if you self-fund your business, you can avoid taking on this debt and the associated costs. This can be especially valuable in the early stages of your business, when cash flow may be tight and you need to conserve resources. By avoiding debt, you'll have more flexibility to invest in your business in other ways, such as hiring new employees or launching new marketing campaigns.

In addition to avoiding debt, self-funding can also help you build a stronger financial foundation for your business over time. When you're not beholden to outside investors or lenders, you can focus on growing your business in a sustainable way, rather than taking on short-term risks in order to meet the expectations of external stakeholders. This can help you build a more resilient business that's better able to weather economic ups and downs, and that's less vulnerable to external factors outside of your control.

It's important to note that self-funding may not be the right choice for all businesses, especially those that require significant upfront investments or that operate in highly competitive markets. In these cases, external funding sources may be necessary in order to achieve your goals and stay competitive. It's important to carefully consider your business's unique needs and priorities when deciding whether or not to pursue self-funding as a strategy.

No equity dilution:

Another advantage of bootstrapping and self-funding is that you can avoid diluting your ownership stake in your business. When you raise funds from external investors, you typically need to give up a portion of your equity in exchange for the capital you receive. This means that you'll own a smaller percentage of your business, which can limit your control over key decisions and potentially even put your leadership position at risk.

By contrast, if you self-fund your business, you can retain full ownership and control over your company. This can be especially valuable if you have a strong vision for your business and want to ensure that you can pursue it without interference from outside parties. It can also be important if you plan to build a long-term business that you hope to pass down to future generations or sell for a significant profit at some point in the future.

In addition to retaining control and ownership, avoiding equity dilution can also help you build a more valuable business over time. When you own a larger percentage of your company, you'll be able to capture a greater share of the profits and reinvest them back into the business. This can help you achieve faster growth, build stronger relationships with customers and suppliers, and ultimately create more value for yourself and your stakeholders.

It's important to note that self-funding may limit your ability to scale your business quickly or pursue larger opportunities. If you're looking to expand rapidly or break into new markets, you may need to bring on external investors or partners to help you achieve your goals. It's important to carefully weigh the pros and cons of different funding strategies based on your specific business needs and goals.

Focus on profitability:

When you self-fund your business, you're forced to focus on profitability from the outset. You don't have the luxury of burning through cash reserves or relying on external funding to cover your losses. Instead, you need to make sure that every dollar you spend is driving revenue and contributing to the bottom line.

This focus on profitability can be a powerful motivator for entrepreneurs. It forces you to be scrappy, creative, and resourceful in finding ways to generate revenue and cut costs. You'll be more inclined to experiment with different business models, test new marketing channels, and optimize your operations to maximize efficiency.

This approach can also help you build a more sustainable business over time. By focusing on profitability early on, you'll be able to reinvest your profits back into the business and fuel continued growth. You'll also be less reliant on external funding, which can be particularly valuable during economic downturns or other periods of financial uncertainty.

However, it's important to recognize that this focus on profitability can also be a double-edged sword. It may mean that you're more risk-averse or less willing to invest in longer-term growth opportunities. You may also need to be more disciplined in managing your cash flow and avoiding unnecessary expenses.

The decision to focus on profitability versus growth will depend on your individual business goals and circumstances. However, by self-funding your business, you can ensure that you're building a business that's both financially sustainable and personally rewarding.

Improved financial management:

Bootstrapping and self-funding can also lead to improved financial management. When you're funding the business yourself, you'll be more invested in tracking your financials and making sure that every dollar is being used effectively. You'll have a better understanding of your cash flow, expenses, and revenue streams, which can help you make more informed decisions about where to allocate resources.

This level of financial management can be particularly valuable when seeking external funding down the line. Investors will be looking for evidence of strong financial discipline and a solid understanding of the business's financials. By demonstrating that you've been able to effectively manage your finances without outside investment, you'll be in a stronger position to negotiate favorable terms with potential investors.

Improved financial management can help you identify potential issues early on and make necessary adjustments. You'll be able to see where your money is going and make informed decisions about whether to cut costs or invest more in certain areas. This can help you avoid running out of cash or getting into debt, which can be particularly challenging for startups and small businesses.

Self-funding can help entrepreneurs develop the financial discipline and management skills necessary for long-term success. By taking ownership of your finances from the outset, you'll be better positioned to make smart, strategic decisions and build a business that's both financially sustainable and profitable.

Bootstrapping and self-funding can be a great way to launch and grow a business without taking on significant debt or giving up equity to outside investors. These approaches can be ideal for entrepreneurs who want to maintain control of their business, or who may not have access to traditional funding sources. While it can be challenging to fund a business using only your own resources, the advantages are many and can lead to long-term success.

3.2 Strategies for reducing costs and maximizing revenue

Bootstrapping and self-funding often require entrepreneurs to be creative and resourceful in finding ways to reduce costs and maximize revenue.

Here are some strategies that can be effective in achieving these goals:

Minimize fixed costs:

Fixed costs are expenses that don't vary based on the volume of sales or production, such as rent, salaries, and utilities. To reduce fixed costs, entrepreneurs can consider sharing office space, outsourcing certain tasks, or hiring part-time or contract workers instead of full-time employees.

Negotiate with vendors:

Entrepreneurs can often negotiate better prices with vendors by leveraging their purchasing power and seeking out discounts or volume pricing.

Increase operational efficiency:

By optimizing processes and streamlining operations, entrepreneurs can reduce the time and resources required to produce and deliver products or services. This can result in cost savings and increased productivity.

Focus on high-margin products or services:

Not all products or services are created equal in terms of profitability. By focusing on those that generate the highest margins, entrepreneurs can maximize revenue and profits.

Expand the customer base:

Increasing the customer base can help generate more revenue and improve cash flow. This can be achieved through targeted marketing campaigns, referral programs, or strategic partnerships.

Explore new revenue streams:

Entrepreneurs can explore new ways to generate revenue by developing complementary products or services, creating new pricing models, or licensing their technology or intellectual property.

By implementing these strategies, entrepreneurs can reduce costs and generate revenue without sacrificing quality or the long-term viability of the business. These skills are not only valuable in the context of bootstrapping and self-funding, but are also important for building a sustainable and successful business over the long term.

3.3 Tips for managing cash flow

Monitor and track expenses:

Keeping track of all expenses, no matter how small, can help entrepreneurs identify areas where they can reduce costs and improve cash flow.

Invoice promptly and follow up on payments:

Promptly invoicing clients and following up on overdue payments can help ensure that cash flows into the business on a consistent basis.

Manage inventory effectively:

Excess inventory ties up cash that could be used for other purposes. By managing inventory effectively and minimizing excess stock, entrepreneurs can free up cash to invest in other areas of the business.

Negotiate payment terms with suppliers:

Negotiating longer payment terms with suppliers can help improve cash flow in the short term, although it's important to balance this with maintaining good relationships with suppliers.

Plan for contingencies:

Unexpected events, such as a downturn in the market or a major customer going out of business, can have a significant impact on cash flow. By planning for contingencies and maintaining a cash reserve, entrepreneurs can better weather these events.

Consider financing options:

While bootstrapping and self-funding may involve avoiding debt, entrepreneurs may still need to consider financing options in certain situations. For example, a short-term loan or line of credit can help bridge a cash flow gap.

By implementing these tips and being proactive about cash flow management, entrepreneurs can ensure that they have the cash they need to grow and succeed over the long term.

3.4 How to know when it's time to seek external funding

Bootstrapping and self-funding can be effective ways to get a business off the ground, but there may come a time when external funding is necessary to take the business to the next level.

Here are some signs that it may be time to seek external funding:

Rapid growth:

If the business is growing quickly and there is a demand for more products or services than the business can currently provide, external funding may be needed to scale the business.

Limited cash flow:

If the business is struggling to manage cash flow and is unable to fund new projects or initiatives, external funding may be necessary to bridge the cash flow gap.

New market opportunities:

If there are new market opportunities that the business is unable to pursue due to lack of resources, external funding may be needed to take advantage of these opportunities.

Capital-intensive projects:

If the business needs to invest in capital-intensive projects, such as new equipment or facilities, external funding may be necessary to finance these projects.

Hiring needs:

If the business needs to hire additional staff to support growth or new initiatives, external funding may be needed to cover the costs of these hires.

Competition:

If the business is facing increased competition and needs to invest in marketing, product development, or other initiatives to remain competitive, external funding may be necessary.

Personal financial strain:

If the business is causing personal financial strain for the entrepreneur, such as by depleting personal savings or causing financial stress on the entrepreneur's family, external funding may be necessary to alleviate this strain.

When considering external funding options, it's important for entrepreneurs to carefully evaluate their options and choose the best fit for their business. This may involve researching different types of funding, such as loans, grants, or equity financing, and considering factors such as interest rates, repayment terms, and potential impact on ownership and control of the business.

Part 4: Traditional Funding Sources

When bootstrapping and self-funding are no longer sufficient to support the growth of a business, traditional funding sources may become necessary. This section of the book will explore the various options available to entrepreneurs seeking external funding from traditional sources, such as banks and other financial institutions. We will discuss the benefits and drawbacks of each option, as well as tips for preparing a successful funding application. Whether you are seeking a loan or line of credit, or exploring other funding options, this section will provide you with the information you need to make informed decisions about traditional funding sources for your business.

4.1 Bank loans

Bank loans are one of the most common forms of traditional funding sources for businesses. They are typically offered by commercial banks, credit unions, and other financial institutions. Bank loans can be secured or unsecured, with the former requiring collateral such as property or equipment to secure the loan.

The advantage of bank loans is that they often come with lower interest rates compared to other types of financing options, making them an attractive option for businesses looking to fund long-term projects. Additionally, banks can often offer flexible repayment terms and repayment schedules that can be tailored to the needs of the borrower.

Bank loans can be difficult to obtain, particularly for small businesses or those with less established credit histories. Banks typically require a thorough review of the borrower's financial history and creditworthiness, as well as collateral to secure the loan. The application process can be time-consuming, and approval is not guaranteed.

In order to increase your chances of obtaining a bank loan, it is important to have a solid business plan in place, a strong credit history, and collateral or assets that can be used to secure the loan. Working with a financial advisor or consultant can also help you prepare a strong loan application and navigate the application process.

4.2 Angel investors

Angel investors are typically high net worth individuals or groups of investors who provide early-stage funding for startups and small businesses in exchange for equity in the company. Unlike traditional lenders such as banks, angel investors are often willing to take on more risk in exchange for potentially higher returns on their investment.

One advantage of angel investors is that they often have industry expertise and can provide valuable guidance and mentorship to the entrepreneur. They may also be willing to provide additional rounds of funding as the company grows and reaches certain milestones.

However, the downside of angel investors is that they typically require a significant ownership stake in the company, which can result in the entrepreneur losing some control over their business. Angel investors also often require a detailed business plan, financial projections, and other documentation before making an investment decision.

To increase your chances of attracting angel investors, it is important to have a solid business plan, a strong management team, and a compelling vision for the future of the company. Building relationships with potential investors through networking events and industry conferences can also be helpful. Working with a professional advisor or consultant who has experience in the angel investing space can also be beneficial in preparing for and negotiating with potential investors.

4.3 Venture capitalists

Venture capitalists (VCs) are investors who provide funding to startups and early-stage businesses that have the potential for high growth and significant returns. Unlike angel investors, VCs are typically institutional investors such as investment banks, private equity firms, and hedge funds.

One of the key advantages of working with a venture capitalist is the amount of funding that can be secured. VCs typically invest larger amounts of money than angel investors or traditional lenders such as banks. Additionally, VCs often bring extensive industry expertise, strategic guidance, and valuable connections to the table.

There are also downsides to working with venture capitalists. VCs often require a significant ownership stake in the company, which can result in the entrepreneur losing some control over their business. Additionally, VCs typically have strict timelines for achieving a return on their investment and may push for a quick exit strategy, such as an IPO or acquisition, which may not align with the entrepreneur's vision for the company.

To attract venture capital funding, it is important to have a compelling business plan, a strong management team, and a clear path to profitability and growth. It is also important to have a thorough understanding of the venture capital industry, including how to identify and target the right investors, as well as the negotiation and due diligence process.

Working with a professional advisor or consultant who has experience in the venture capital industry can be invaluable in preparing for and negotiating with potential investors. It is also important to carefully consider the terms and conditions of any funding offer before accepting, to ensure that it aligns with the long-term goals and vision for the company.

4.4 Pros and cons of traditional funding sources

4.4.1 Pros

- Availability of larger funding amounts: Traditional funding sources such as bank loans, angel investors, and venture capitalists often have deeper pockets and can provide larger funding amounts compared to bootstrapping or self-funding.

- Expertise and network: Investors from traditional funding sources often come with a wealth of experience and a vast network of industry contacts that can benefit a business in the long run.

- Credibility: Securing funding from traditional sources can help to build a business's credibility and improve its reputation within the industry.

- Access to mentorship: In addition to funding, investors from traditional sources often offer mentorship to the businesses they fund. This can be invaluable for a business that is just starting out or looking to grow.

4.4.2 Cons

- Loss of control: Accepting funding from traditional sources often means giving up some degree of control over the business to the investors. This can include decisions on strategy, management, and even the direction of the company.

- High competition: Traditional funding sources are often highly competitive, with many businesses vying for limited funding opportunities. This can make it difficult for some businesses to secure funding, particularly those that are just starting out or are in less popular industries.

- Time-consuming: Securing funding from traditional sources often requires a lengthy application process and due diligence from the investors. This can take up valuable time and resources for a business that may need to focus on other areas of the business.

- Equity dilution: Accepting funding from investors often means giving up a percentage of the company's equity, which can dilute the ownership of the founders and other shareholders.

It's important to carefully consider the pros and cons of each traditional funding source before making a decision on which one to pursue.

Part 5: Alternative Funding Sources

While traditional funding sources like bank loans, angel investors, and venture capitalists are popular choices for financing a business, there are also many alternative funding sources available. These sources may be particularly attractive to entrepreneurs who are unable to secure traditional funding or who are seeking more flexible financing options. In this section, we'll explore several alternative funding sources that entrepreneurs can consider, including crowdfunding, peer-to-peer lending, and grants. We'll discuss how these funding sources work, their advantages and disadvantages, and tips for successfully securing funding from these sources.

5.1 Crowdfunding

Crowdfunding has become a popular way for entrepreneurs to raise money for their businesses. It involves soliciting funds from a large number of people, often through an online platform. Crowdfunding campaigns can take many forms, such as rewards-based crowdfunding or equity crowdfunding.

Rewards-based crowdfunding involves offering a product or service in exchange for funding. For example, an entrepreneur might offer pre-orders of their product or exclusive access to their service to those who contribute to their crowdfunding campaign. Equity crowdfunding, on the other hand, involves selling shares of the business to investors through an online platform.

One of the biggest advantages of crowdfunding is that it can provide entrepreneurs with access to a large pool of potential investors who are interested in supporting innovative ideas. Additionally, crowdfunding campaigns can help businesses build a community of supporters who are invested in the success of the company.

However, there are also some disadvantages to crowdfunding. It can be time-consuming and challenging to create a successful campaign that generates significant funding. Additionally, entrepreneurs who choose equity crowdfunding may be giving up some control over their business by selling shares to outside investors.

Overall, crowdfunding can be a useful alternative funding source for entrepreneurs who are willing to put in the time and effort to create a compelling campaign and build a community of supporters.

5.2 Peer-to-peer lending

Peer-to-peer lending, also known as P2P lending or social lending, is a form of alternative funding where individuals lend money to other individuals or businesses through online platforms. This type of funding allows borrowers to access financing without having to go through traditional financial institutions like banks.

One of the main advantages of P2P lending is that it provides borrowers with access to capital that they might not have been able to obtain through traditional lending channels. Additionally, P2P lending often offers lower interest rates compared to traditional bank loans, which can be especially beneficial for small businesses and individuals with limited credit histories.

On the other hand, P2P lending also comes with certain risks. Since it involves borrowing from individuals rather than banks, there is a higher risk of default, and investors may not receive their full investment back. Additionally, P2P lending platforms may not be as tightly regulated as traditional financial institutions, which can lead to potential fraud or misuse of funds.

P2P lending can be a viable option for businesses and individuals looking for alternative sources of funding, but it's important to carefully consider the risks and benefits before pursuing this type of financing.

5.3 Grants and government funding

Grants and government funding are alternative funding sources that can provide significant financial support to businesses. Grants are typically awarded by government agencies or private organizations to businesses that meet certain criteria, such as working in a specific industry or addressing a particular social or environmental issue.

One of the main advantages of grants is that they do not need to be repaid, which can be a major relief for businesses that are struggling to make ends meet. Additionally, grants can provide access to funding that might not be available through traditional sources, and they can often be used for specific purposes, such as research and development or environmental sustainability.

Government funding is another option for businesses looking for alternative sources of funding. This can include loans, loan guarantees, or direct investments from government agencies. In some cases, government funding may be available for specific industries or projects that align with government priorities, such as renewable energy or infrastructure development.

One potential drawback of grants and government funding is that they can be highly competitive, with many businesses vying for a limited pool of resources. Additionally, there may be strict eligibility requirements or reporting requirements that businesses must adhere to in order to maintain their funding.

Grants and government funding can be a valuable source of financing for businesses, but they require careful research and planning to determine if they are the right fit for a particular business's needs and goals.

5.4 Pros and cons of alternative funding sources

Pros:

- Access to capital: Alternative funding sources provide entrepreneurs with additional avenues to obtain the capital they need to start or grow their business.

- Lower interest rates: Depending on the source of funding, alternative funding may come with lower interest rates than traditional sources such as bank loans.

- Diversification: By using alternative funding sources, entrepreneurs can diversify their funding streams, reducing their dependence on any one source of capital.

- Flexibility: Alternative funding sources may offer more flexible terms than traditional funding sources, such as more forgiving repayment schedules or lower collateral requirements.

Cons:

- Limited availability: Alternative funding sources may not be available in all regions or for all types of businesses.

- Higher risk: Because alternative funding sources often cater to riskier ventures, they may come with higher interest rates or stricter repayment terms.

- Crowded marketplace: Some alternative funding sources, such as crowdfunding platforms, can be highly competitive, making it difficult for businesses to stand out and secure funding.

- Limited control: Depending on the source of funding, entrepreneurs may have to give up some control over their business or accept specific conditions or restrictions.

It's important to carefully consider the pros and cons of alternative funding sources before deciding whether they are the right fit for your business.

Part 6: Pitching to Investors

Pitching to investors can be a crucial step in securing funding for your business. Whether you're seeking funding from traditional sources like venture capitalists or angel investors, or exploring alternative funding options like crowdfunding or peer-to-peer lending, the success of your pitch can make or break your chances of securing the investment you need.

In this section, we'll cover everything you need to know about crafting a compelling pitch that showcases your business in the best possible light. We'll explore the key elements of a successful pitch, from the elevator pitch to the full-length presentation, and provide tips for tailoring your pitch to different types of investors and funding sources. Whether you're a seasoned entrepreneur or a first-time founder, the insights and strategies in this section will help you build the confidence and skills you need to deliver a winning pitch.

6.1 What investors look for in a pitch

Strong value proposition:

Investors want to see a compelling and unique value proposition that sets your business apart from competitors. Your pitch should clearly explain how your product or service solves a problem or fulfills a need in the market.

Market opportunity:

Investors want to see that there is a sizable and growing market for your product or service. You should demonstrate a deep understanding of your target market and show how your business has the potential to capture a significant share of that market.

Experienced team:

Investors want to see that your team has the experience and expertise necessary to execute on your business plan. You should highlight the relevant experience of your team members and explain how their skills and knowledge will contribute to the success of the business.

Traction and milestones:

Investors want to see that your business has made progress and achieved significant milestones. You should be able to demonstrate that your product or service has gained traction in the market and that you have a clear roadmap for future growth.

Financials:

Investors want to see that your business is financially viable and has a clear path to profitability. Your pitch should include detailed financial projections and explain how you plan to generate revenue and manage costs.

Clear ask:

Finally, investors want to know what you are asking for and how the funding will be used. You should clearly state how much funding you are seeking, what the funds will be used for, and what investors can expect in return (such as equity or a return on investment).

6.2 Developing a strong pitch deck

Developing a strong pitch deck is an essential part of successfully pitching to investors. A pitch deck is a visual aid that outlines the key points of your business plan and captures the attention of potential investors.

Here are some tips for creating a strong pitch deck:

Start with a strong introduction:

The first few slides of your pitch deck should grab the investor's attention and clearly communicate your value proposition.

Keep it simple and focused:

Avoid cluttering your pitch deck with too much information. Focus on the key points of your business plan, such as your market opportunity, team, and financial projections.

Use visuals:

Visuals such as graphs, charts, and images can help make your pitch deck more engaging and easier to understand.
Highlight your unique selling proposition: Make it clear what sets your business apart from competitors.

Address potential risks:

Investors want to know that you have thought about potential risks and have a plan to mitigate them.

End with a strong call to action:

End your pitch deck with a clear call to action, such as a request for a meeting or follow-up conversation.

Remember, your pitch deck is a tool to support your pitch, not a replacement for it. You should be prepared to speak to each slide in detail and answer any questions that investors may have.

6.3 Strategies for delivering an effective pitch

Here are some strategies for delivering an effective pitch:

Be prepared:

Practice your pitch multiple times, and make sure you have a deep understanding of your business and its unique value proposition. Be ready to answer any questions that may arise.

Start with a hook:

Capture the investors' attention with a strong opening that highlights your business's most compelling feature.

Keep it concise:

Investors have limited attention spans, so make sure your pitch is clear and to the point. A good rule of thumb is to keep your pitch deck to no more than 10-12 slides.

Use visual aids:

Use visuals such as graphs, charts, and images to help illustrate your points and keep the investors engaged.

Show market opportunity:

Investors want to know that there is a sizable market opportunity for your product or service. Be sure to include data and research that supports your claims.

Highlight your team:

Investors not only invest in the product or service but also the team behind it. Make sure to showcase the relevant experience and expertise of your team members.

Address risks and challenges:

No business is without risks and challenges. Be upfront about the potential obstacles your business may face and how you plan to overcome them.

End with a call to action:

End your pitch with a clear call to action, whether it's asking for funding or a follow-up meeting.

By following these strategies, you can increase the likelihood of delivering an effective pitch that resonates with potential investors.

6.4 Handling questions and objections from investors

Once you have delivered your pitch, it is common for investors to have questions and objections. It is important to be prepared to handle these in a professional and confident manner.
Here are some tips for handling questions and objections:

Listen carefully:

When an entrepreneur is pitching to investors, it's important to remember that investors will often have questions or objections. As such, it's crucial to listen carefully to what they are saying in order to fully understand their concerns and respond appropriately. Sometimes, entrepreneurs may be so focused on delivering their pitch that they may not fully hear or understand the questions being asked. This can lead to misunderstandings and missed opportunities.

One effective strategy for listening carefully is to repeat the question or objection back to the investor in your own words. This not only helps you to fully understand the question, but it also shows the investor that you are actively listening and taking their concerns seriously.

Another important aspect of listening carefully is to be open to feedback and constructive criticism. Investors are often experienced business professionals who can offer valuable insights and perspectives. It's important to take their feedback into consideration and use it to improve your pitch and your business overall.

Investors may also ask questions or make objections that you simply don't have an answer for. In these situations, it's important to be honest and transparent. You can always promise to follow up with more information or to research the issue further. This shows that you are committed to providing accurate and thorough information and that you value the investor's input.

Stay calm:

When pitching to investors, it is important to stay calm and composed, even when facing tough questions or objections. This can be easier said than done, as pitching can be a nerve-wracking experience, but it is crucial to maintain a professional demeanor.

Staying calm shows that you have confidence in your business and your ability to handle difficult situations. It also demonstrates that you are capable of thinking on your feet and addressing issues as they arise.

One way to stay calm is to practice your pitch in advance and prepare for potential questions or objections. This can help you feel more confident and in control during the actual presentation. It may also be helpful to take deep breaths and stay focused on your main points.

Investors are not trying to attack you personally or tear down your business. They are simply trying to assess whether your business is a good investment opportunity. By staying calm and addressing their concerns thoughtfully, you can increase your chances of success in securing funding.

Be honest:

Being honest is a crucial aspect of handling questions and objections from investors during a pitch. It can be tempting to exaggerate or conceal certain aspects of the business to make it appear more attractive to investors. However, this can ultimately backfire and damage the credibility and trustworthiness of the founder and the business.

When an investor asks a tough question or raises an objection, it is important to acknowledge the concern and answer it honestly. If there is an issue or challenge in the business, it is better to address it upfront and provide a clear plan for addressing it. This demonstrates that the founder has a realistic understanding of the business and is proactive in addressing potential challenges.

Being honest can also help to build a stronger relationship with investors in the long run. Investors appreciate transparency and honesty, and are more likely to continue to support a business that is open and upfront about its challenges and limitations. It also sets a positive tone for future interactions and can help to establish a foundation of trust between the founder and the investor.

Address the underlying concern:

When an investor raises an objection or asks a challenging question during a pitch, it's important to address their underlying concern rather than simply trying to provide a surface-level answer. This means taking the time to understand what is driving their question or objection and responding in a thoughtful and honest manner.

To do this effectively, you may need to ask clarifying questions to get a better understanding of their perspective. Once you have a clear idea of their concerns, you can then address them directly and offer evidence or information that supports your position.

It's also important to avoid becoming defensive or dismissive of their concerns. Instead, acknowledge the validity of their perspective and use it as an opportunity to demonstrate your expertise and knowledge of the market and your business.

By addressing underlying concerns in a thoughtful and honest way, you can help to build trust and credibility with potential investors and increase the likelihood of securing funding for your business.

Practice:

practicing is essential when it comes to delivering an effective pitch and handling questions from investors. It can help you refine your message and anticipate potential objections.

One way to practice is by rehearsing your pitch in front of friends, family, or colleagues and asking for feedback. This can help you identify areas that need improvement and gain confidence in your delivery.

Another useful strategy is to participate in pitch competitions or attend networking events where you can practice pitching to a live audience. These opportunities can also provide valuable feedback and help you develop relationships with potential investors.

It's also essential to prepare for potential questions and objections that investors may have. Research the backgrounds and investment preferences of the investors you plan to pitch to and try to anticipate their concerns. This can help you address potential objections in your pitch and show that you've done your homework.

Practice makes perfect, and the more you rehearse your pitch and anticipate potential objections, the better prepared you'll be to deliver an effective pitch and secure funding for your business.

Handling questions and objections effectively can make a big difference in the outcome of your pitch. Be prepared, stay calm, and respond thoughtfully and honestly.

Part 7: Closing the Deal

Part 7 of the book focuses on the final steps in securing funding for your business, which involve negotiating and closing the deal with investors. This section will explore the key considerations involved in finalizing funding arrangements, including the legal and financial aspects of the process. Additionally, it will provide tips for negotiating favorable terms for both you and your investors, and discuss how to ensure a smooth and successful funding round closure.

7.1 Negotiating deal terms

negotiating deal terms is a critical aspect of closing the deal with investors. Once a potential investor has expressed interest in funding your business, the negotiations begin. It's essential to have a good understanding of the terms being offered, the market rate for similar investments, and what you are willing to concede to secure the funding. Both parties need to be clear on what they expect from the deal and negotiate to find common ground.

Some of the critical deal terms to negotiate include the amount of funding, equity stake, valuation, board seats, voting rights, dividends, and exit clauses. It's essential to have a clear understanding of what you're willing to give up and what you're not willing to negotiate on. It's also important to be flexible and willing to compromise to reach an agreement that works for both parties.

Negotiations can take time and require a lot of back and forth communication. It's important to have open and transparent communication with the investor to ensure that everyone is on the same page. In the end, the goal is to create a mutually beneficial agreement that meets the needs of both parties and sets the stage for a successful partnership.

7.2 Protecting your business interests

When closing a funding deal, it is important to ensure that your business interests are protected. This involves negotiating the terms of the deal in a way that balances the needs of the investor with the needs of your business. One important consideration is the valuation of your company, which will determine how much equity you will need to give up in exchange for funding. Other key terms to consider include the amount of funding being offered, the length of the funding agreement, the interest rate and any associated fees, and any equity or ownership rights granted to the investor.

To protect your interests, it is important to carefully review and negotiate the terms of the agreement. This may involve seeking legal advice to ensure that the terms are fair and reasonable. It is also important to ensure that any legal documents, such as shareholder agreements or operating agreements, are properly drafted and reflect the terms of the deal.

Another important consideration is the potential impact of the funding on the day-to-day operations of your business. It is important to consider how the funding will be used and to have a clear plan in place for managing the funds effectively. This may involve developing a budget and financial plan, as well as establishing clear communication channels with the investor to ensure that everyone is on the same page.

Closing a funding deal requires careful negotiation and planning to ensure that your business interests are protected. By taking the time to carefully review and negotiate the terms of the agreement, you can ensure that your business is well-positioned for long-term success.

7.3 Legal considerations when accepting funding

When accepting funding, it is important for entrepreneurs to consider the legal implications and obligations that come with it. Some legal considerations to keep in mind include:

Investment agreements:

Investment agreements are legal documents that outline the terms and conditions of an investment deal between the entrepreneur and the investor. These agreements typically include details about the amount of funding being provided, the percentage of ownership that the investor will receive in exchange for the funding, the expected return on investment, and the rights and responsibilities of both parties.

Some common components of investment agreements include:

Valuation:

The valuation of the company is an important consideration in investment agreements. Investors will typically want a fair valuation of the company that reflects its current worth, potential for growth, and competitive landscape.

Equity:

Investors may receive equity in the company in exchange for their funding. The amount of equity will depend on the amount of funding provided, the valuation of the company, and the negotiated terms of the investment.

Board membership:

Some investors may require a seat on the company's board of directors as part of their investment agreement. This can provide them with additional oversight and influence over the direction of the company.

Investor rights:

Investment agreements may include provisions that protect the rights of the investor, such as anti-dilution clauses that prevent the entrepreneur from issuing additional shares that would dilute the investor's ownership stake.

Exit strategy: Investment agreements may also include details about the exit strategy for the investor. This may include provisions for the entrepreneur to buy back the investor's shares, a requirement for the company to go public, or an agreement to sell the company within a certain timeframe.

Investment agreements are complex legal documents that require careful consideration and negotiation. It is important for entrepreneurs to seek the advice of a qualified attorney before entering into any investment agreement to ensure that their interests are protected.

Intellectual property:

Intellectual property (IP) is a critical consideration when accepting funding, as it represents the intangible assets that give your business a competitive advantage. These assets can include patents, trademarks, copyrights, trade secrets, and more. It's essential to protect your IP to ensure that you maintain ownership and control over it, and that others can't use or profit from it without your permission.

When negotiating funding agreements, you should consider including provisions that address IP ownership, use, and protection. For example, you may want to require that the investor or lender sign a nondisclosure agreement (NDA) before sharing any sensitive information about your business, to prevent them from sharing it with others or using it for their own purposes.

You should also consider registering your IP with the relevant authorities, such as the US Patent and Trademark Office (USPTO) or the World Intellectual Property Organization (WIPO), to establish your ownership rights and prevent others from using or infringing on your IP.

You should work with an attorney to ensure that your funding agreements include provisions that address IP ownership and use, as well as any restrictions on the use or disclosure of your confidential information. This can help protect your business interests and ensure that your IP remains a valuable asset that can help your business grow and succeed.

Regulatory compliance:

Regulatory compliance refers to the process of ensuring that a company adheres to all the relevant laws and regulations in its industry. This is an important consideration when accepting funding, as non-compliance can result in significant legal and financial penalties.

One area of regulatory compliance that startups should pay particular attention to is data privacy. This is becoming an increasingly important issue, with regulations such as the European Union's General Data Protection Regulation (GDPR) and California's Consumer Privacy Act (CCPA) imposing strict rules on how companies collect, use, and protect personal data. Startups should ensure that they have robust data privacy policies in place and that they are following best practices for data protection.

Another area of regulatory compliance to consider is industry-specific regulations. For example, if you are in the healthcare industry, you may be subject to regulations such as HIPAA (Health Insurance Portability and Accountability Act) that govern how patient data is handled. If you are in the financial industry, you may need to comply with regulations such as the Sarbanes-Oxley Act or the Dodd-Frank Act. It's important to research and understand the regulations that apply to your industry and ensure that you are in compliance.

Failing to comply with regulations can result in fines, legal action, and reputational damage. It's important to take regulatory compliance seriously and ensure that your startup is doing everything it can to comply with all applicable laws and regulations.

Tax implications:

When accepting funding, it's important to consider the tax implications for your business. Depending on the type of funding and how it's structured, you may be required to pay taxes on the funding received.

For example, if you receive a loan, you will need to pay interest on the loan, which may be tax-deductible. If you receive equity funding, you may be subject to capital gains tax if you sell your shares at a profit.
It's important to consult with a tax professional to understand the specific tax implications of the funding you're receiving and to ensure that you're complying with all applicable tax laws and regulations. Failure to do so can result in penalties and legal issues down the line.

Disclosure requirements:

Disclosure requirements refer to the legal obligations of a business to disclose certain information to its investors or potential investors. This information can include financial statements, business plans, risk factors, legal disputes, and any other material information that could affect an investor's decision to invest.

When accepting funding, it is important to be aware of the disclosure requirements in your jurisdiction. In the United States, for example, the Securities and Exchange Commission (SEC) requires companies to register their securities offerings and file periodic reports with the agency.

These reports, such as Form 10-K and Form 10-Q, provide detailed financial and operational information to investors and the public.

In addition to legal requirements, it is also important to consider the ethical and reputational implications of disclosure. Investors expect transparency and honesty from the businesses they invest in, and failure to disclose material information can result in legal and financial consequences, as well as damage to the company's reputation.

It is recommended to consult with legal and financial professionals to ensure that all disclosure requirements are met and that the company is presenting accurate and complete information to potential investors.

By keeping these legal considerations in mind, entrepreneurs can protect their businesses and ensure that they are in compliance with all relevant laws and regulations when accepting funding.

7.4 Closing the deal and moving forward

Closing the deal is an important milestone for any entrepreneur seeking funding. This is the point at which the investor commits to investing in the business and the entrepreneur agrees to the terms of the investment. Once the deal is closed, both parties must work together to move the business forward.

The closing process involves several steps, including finalizing the investment agreement, transferring funds, and filing necessary paperwork with regulatory agencies. The entrepreneur should work closely with legal and financial professionals to ensure that all aspects of the deal are handled properly and in compliance with relevant laws and regulations.

It is important to note that closing the deal is not the end of the process. Once funding is secured, the entrepreneur must work diligently to build the business and achieve the goals set out in the business plan. The investor will likely want to be kept informed of the company's progress and may have certain expectations for growth and profitability.

It is also important for the entrepreneur to maintain a good relationship with the investor. This may involve regular communication, providing updates on the company's progress, and seeking guidance and advice when needed. With a strong relationship in place, the investor can become a valuable asset to the business, providing support, connections, and resources to help the entrepreneur achieve success.

Part 8: Managing Funds and Growing Your Business

Congratulations! You have successfully secured funding for your business. However, the hard work is far from over. The next step is to effectively manage those funds and grow your business to achieve the goals set out in your business plan. This is where Part 8 of our guide comes in.

Managing funds is a critical part of building a successful business. It requires careful planning, financial discipline, and effective use of resources. In this section, we will discuss various strategies and tools to help you manage your funds, including creating a budget, monitoring cash flow, and tracking expenses.

Growing your business is equally important. With the right strategies and tactics, you can increase your customer base, expand your product offerings, and ultimately increase revenue and profitability. We will cover topics such as marketing and sales strategies, product development, and scaling your business.

Remember, managing funds and growing your business are ongoing processes. It requires constant evaluation and adjustment to ensure that you are on track to achieve your goals. With the right approach and a commitment to excellence, you can build a successful and sustainable business.

8.1 How to effectively manage funds

Managing funds effectively is crucial for any business, particularly for those that have secured funding from external sources. Here are some tips for managing funds effectively:

Develop a budget:

A budget is a plan that outlines your expected income and expenses. It is important to develop a budget for your business to ensure that you are spending within your means and that you have enough funds to cover all your expenses.

Monitor your cash flow:

Cash flow is the amount of cash that is coming in and going out of your business. Monitoring your cash flow regularly will help you to identify any cash flow issues early on and take corrective action.

Keep accurate financial records:

Keeping accurate financial records is crucial for managing funds effectively. You should keep track of all your income and expenses, and ensure that all transactions are properly recorded.

Seek professional advice:

If you are not experienced in financial management, it is a good idea to seek advice from a financial professional. They can help you develop a budget, monitor your cash flow, and keep accurate financial records.

Use technology:

There are many financial management tools available that can help you manage your funds effectively. These tools can help you monitor your cash flow, keep track of your expenses, and generate financial reports.

By following these tips, you can effectively manage your funds and ensure that your business remains financially healthy.

8.2 Strategies for scaling your business

Once funding has been secured and the business is up and running, it is important for entrepreneurs to focus on strategies for scaling and growing the business. Scaling a business involves expanding its operations and increasing its revenue, without sacrificing quality or losing focus on core values.

One key strategy for scaling a business is to focus on customer acquisition and retention. Entrepreneurs should identify their target market and develop effective marketing and sales strategies to reach them. They should also focus on providing excellent customer service and building strong relationships with their customers, which can lead to repeat business and positive word-of-mouth marketing.

Another important strategy for scaling a business is to focus on operational efficiency. Entrepreneurs should continually evaluate and optimize their processes and systems to streamline operations and reduce costs. This may involve automating certain tasks, outsourcing non-core functions, and implementing technology solutions to improve productivity and efficiency.

Entrepreneurs should also focus on building a strong team to support growth and expansion. This involves hiring talented and experienced employees who share the company's values and vision, and providing them with the necessary training and resources to succeed.

Entrepreneurs should be willing to take calculated risks in order to drive growth and expansion. This may involve launching new products or services, entering new markets, or pursuing strategic partnerships or acquisitions. However, these risks should always be carefully evaluated and aligned with the company's overall goals and values.

8.3 Common pitfalls to avoid when growing your business

Lack of focus:

Entrepreneurs often have many ideas and opportunities, but it is important to remain focused on the core business and avoid distractions that can derail progress.

Failure to adapt:

The business landscape is constantly evolving, and entrepreneurs must be willing to adapt to changing market conditions, technologies, and customer preferences in order to stay competitive.

Overexpansion:

Rapid growth can be tempting, but it is important to ensure that the business has the resources, infrastructure, and systems in place to support expansion without sacrificing quality or customer service.

Poor financial management:

Effective financial management is crucial for the success of any business. Entrepreneurs must ensure that they have accurate financial records, manage cash flow effectively, and make informed decisions based on financial data.

Ineffective team management:

Building a strong team is essential for the growth and success of a business. Entrepreneurs must be able to attract and retain top talent, communicate effectively with team members, and provide opportunities for professional growth and development.

Lack of innovation:

In order to stay ahead of the competition, entrepreneurs must continually innovate and find new ways to add value for customers. Failure to do so can lead to stagnation and decline.

By being aware of these common pitfalls and taking proactive steps to avoid them, entrepreneurs can increase their chances of success and achieve their goals for growth and expansion.

8.4 Balancing growth with profitability

Balancing growth with profitability is a crucial aspect of managing funds and growing a business. While growth is important for long-term success, it can also be expensive, requiring significant investments in marketing, hiring, and infrastructure. In order to sustain this growth, it is important for the business to generate enough revenue and profits to cover these expenses.

One way to balance growth and profitability is to focus on maximizing efficiency and productivity. This may involve streamlining processes, reducing waste, and leveraging technology to automate tasks and increase output. By operating more efficiently, the business can generate more revenue with less overhead, allowing for more sustainable growth.

Another important strategy is to carefully manage cash flow. This involves keeping a close eye on expenses, billing and collecting payments in a timely manner, and maintaining sufficient reserves to cover unexpected expenses or dips in revenue. By managing cash flow effectively, the business can avoid cash shortages that can impede growth or lead to financial distress.

It is also important to be strategic about growth initiatives, prioritizing investments that are most likely to generate a return on investment. This may involve conducting market research to identify the most promising opportunities for growth, as well as carefully analyzing the costs and benefits of each investment.

Balancing growth with profitability requires careful planning, execution, and monitoring. By taking a disciplined and strategic approach, businesses can achieve sustainable growth while also maintaining a strong financial foundation.

Supporting sections:

In addition to the main sections of this guide, there are several supporting sections that provide additional resources and information for entrepreneurs seeking funding. These sections include a glossary of key terms, a list of funding resources and directories, tips for improving your credit score, and advice on building a strong business plan. Each of these sections can be a valuable tool in helping entrepreneurs navigate the complex world of funding and grow their businesses.

Glossary of funding-related terms

Here are some common funding-related terms that entrepreneurs may encounter during the funding process:

- Angel Investor: A high net worth individual who invests in early-stage startups.
- Burn Rate: The rate at which a company is spending its cash reserves to finance operations.
- Due Diligence: A comprehensive investigation into the financial and legal history of a company, conducted by investors or potential acquirers.
- Exit Strategy: A plan for how investors will eventually sell their stake in the company and realize a return on their investment.
- IPO (Initial Public Offering): The first time a company offers shares of its stock to the public.
- Seed Funding: The initial funding round for a startup, often provided by friends and family or angel investors.
- Series A, B, C, etc.: Subsequent rounds of funding as a startup grows and requires additional capital to scale.
- Term Sheet: A non-binding document outlining the key terms and conditions of a proposed investment deal.
- Valuation: The estimated worth of a company, often determined by factors such as revenue, assets, and market share.
- Vesting: The process by which founders and employees earn ownership in the company over time, typically through stock options or equity grants.

Understanding these and other funding-related terms can help entrepreneurs navigate the funding process and negotiate more effectively with investors.

Case studies of successful businesses and their funding journeys

Case studies of successful businesses and their funding journeys can provide valuable insights and inspiration for entrepreneurs who are seeking funding for their own ventures. These case studies can help to illustrate the various funding sources and strategies that successful businesses have used, as well as the challenges and opportunities that they faced along the way.

By examining the experiences of successful businesses, entrepreneurs can learn about the importance of having a solid business plan, building a strong team, and establishing a clear vision for growth and expansion. They can also gain insights into the types of funding sources that may be most appropriate for their own ventures, as well as the pitfalls and challenges to watch out for.

Some examples of successful businesses and their funding journeys include:

- Airbnb, which raised more than $4 billion in venture capital funding to become one of the world's largest online marketplaces for vacation rentals.
- Warby Parker, which raised $215 million in venture capital funding to disrupt the eyewear industry with its innovative online retail model.
- Tesla, which raised more than $19 billion in equity and debt financing to develop and manufacture electric vehicles and other sustainable energy products.
- Dropbox, which raised more than $1.7 billion in venture capital funding to become one of the world's most popular cloud storage and file sharing services.

These case studies and others can be found in various resources such as business publications, case study collections, and online forums.

Q&A with successful entrepreneurs and investors

Q&A with successful entrepreneurs and investors can be an incredibly valuable resource for those seeking funding and looking to grow their businesses. These Q&A sessions often involve entrepreneurs sharing their personal experiences with funding, discussing challenges they faced, and offering advice and insights based on their own journeys.

Investors can also provide valuable perspectives on what they look for in potential investment opportunities, as well as tips for entrepreneurs on how to effectively pitch and negotiate deals.

In these Q&A sessions, entrepreneurs and investors may discuss a wide range of topics, such as market trends, industry-specific challenges, and strategies for managing funds and growing a business. Attendees can often ask questions and engage in discussions, providing an opportunity to gain valuable insights and connect with others in the startup community.

Q&A sessions with successful entrepreneurs and investors can be an excellent way to learn from those who have been there before and to gain valuable advice and guidance for your own funding and growth journey.

Additional resources and further reading

In addition to the information presented in this guide, there are numerous resources available for entrepreneurs looking to learn more about funding and growing their businesses. This section provides a list of additional resources and further reading, including books, articles, websites, and other tools that can help entrepreneurs navigate the complex world of business funding and management.

Some useful resources for entrepreneurs include:

- The Small Business Administration (SBA): The SBA offers a range of resources for small businesses, including funding programs, educational materials, and networking opportunities.
- SCORE: SCORE is a nonprofit organization that provides free mentoring, training, and resources to small business owners.
- AngelList: AngelList is a platform that connects startups with investors and job seekers. The site also offers resources and information for entrepreneurs looking to raise funding.
- Crunchbase: Crunchbase is a database of startups, investors, and funding rounds that can help entrepreneurs research potential investors and competitors.
- Inc. Magazine: Inc. is a publication that offers articles, videos, and other resources for entrepreneurs and small business owners.
- Entrepreneur: Entrepreneur is a magazine and website that provides resources and information for entrepreneurs at all stages of business development.
- The Lean Startup by Eric Ries: This book provides a framework for building and growing startups in a lean and efficient way.
- Venture Deals by Brad Feld and Jason Mendelson: This book offers a comprehensive guide to the venture capital funding process.
- The Art of Possibility by Rosamund Stone Zander and Benjamin Zander: This book explores the mindset and strategies needed to achieve success in business and in life.

These resources are just a few examples of the many tools and sources of information available to entrepreneurs. By staying informed and taking advantage of available resources, entrepreneurs can increase their chances of success in the competitive world of business.

Conclusion

In conclusion, securing funding for a business can be a challenging and complex process, but it is a critical step in the journey to success. This book has provided a comprehensive guide to navigating the world of funding, from identifying funding sources to pitching to investors and managing funds for growth.

Entrepreneurs must be prepared to do their due diligence, research and plan for the type of funding that suits their business goals and needs. This involves understanding the different types of funding available, such as venture capital, angel investing, crowdfunding, and traditional bank loans, and their pros and cons. It also involves developing a strong business plan, financial projections, and a pitch deck that can effectively communicate the potential of the business to investors.

Once funding is secured, entrepreneurs must effectively manage the funds and make strategic decisions to grow their business while balancing profitability. This involves implementing effective financial management strategies, developing and scaling the business, and avoiding common pitfalls that can derail progress.

Throughout this book, we have emphasized the importance of building strong relationships with investors and maintaining transparent communication. Entrepreneurs must also be aware of legal and regulatory considerations, such as tax implications and intellectual property protection, when accepting funding.

In addition to practical advice and strategies, this book also provides valuable case studies of successful businesses and their funding journeys, as well as Q&A with successful entrepreneurs and investors. These resources offer real-world examples and insights into what it takes to succeed in securing funding and growing a business.

It is important to remember that securing funding is not a guarantee of success. Entrepreneurs must be willing to put in the hard work, adapt to changing circumstances, and stay focused on their goals to achieve success in the long run.

We hope this book has provided you with the knowledge, tools, and resources needed to successfully navigate the funding landscape and build a successful business. Remember to stay informed, seek guidance when needed, and remain persistent in your pursuit of success.

www.ingramcontent.com/pod-product-compliance
Lightning Source LLC
Chambersburg PA
CBHW080620220526
45466CB00010B/3409